RUGBY FOCUS
TEAMWORK AND TACTICS

Jon Richards

First published in 2015 by Wayland

Copyright © Wayland 2015

Dewey Number: 796.3'332-dc22
ISBN: 978 0 7502 9480 5
Library ebook ISBN: 978 0 7502 7666 5

10 9 8 7 6 5 4 3 2 1

MIX
Paper from
responsible sources
FSC® C104740

Editor: Camilla Lloyd
Produced by Tall Tree Ltd
Editor, Tall Tree: Jennifer Sanderson
Designer: Ben Ruocco
Consultant: Tony Buchanan

Wayland
An imprint of
Hachette Children's Group
Part of Hodder & Stoughton
Carmelite House
50 Victoria Embankment
London EC4Y 0DZ

Printed in China

An Hachette UK Company

www.hachette.co.uk

www.hachettechildrens.co.uk

Acknowledgements
The author and publisher would like to thank the
following people for their help and participation
in this book: Old Albanian RFC and Neil Dekker.

Picture credits
All photographs by Michael Wicks except:
(t – top, l – left, r – right, b – bottom, c – centre)
1, 14, 15t Titziana Casalta/Dreamstime.com; 2, 7, 8,
12, 19, 22, 26, 28, 30 Santamaradona/Dreamstime.com;
5 Dgoodings/Dreamstime.com; 6, 18 Grosremy/
Dreamstime.com; 9 Alfredo Falcone/Dreamstime.com;
10 Tatiana Belova/Dreamstime.com; 11, 17t Graphitec/
Dreamstime.com

CONTENTS

A team game

Rugby is a team sport where 15 players work as a unit to score more points than the opposition. Players have to move the ball up the pitch in a co-ordinated way so that they can outmanoeuvre their opponents.

Playing positions

Rugby teams are divided into two groups – forwards and backs. Forwards are usually involved in moves that restart matches, such as scrums (see pages 22–23) and lineouts (see pages 24–25). They are also involved in the period immediately following a tackle, known as a break-down, in rucks and mauls (see pages 18–19). Backs play in attacking moves, and defensive moves to stop opposition attacks.

In a rugby team, the forwards wear numbers one to eight while the backs are numbers 9 to 15.

BALL IN HAND

Different positions are sometimes known by different names. For example, the second row players are sometimes called locks, and the scrum-half and fly-half are sometimes called the half-backs.

1. **Prop (front row)**
2. **Hooker (front row)**
3. **Prop (front row)**
4. **Second row**
5. **Second row**
6. **Flanker (back row)**
7. **Flanker (back row)**
8. **Number eight (back row)**
9. **Scrum-half**
10. **Fly-half**
11. **Left wing**
12. **Centre**
13. **Centre**
14. **Right wing**
15. **Full back**

Leicester scrum-half, Ben Youngs, passes the ball during a game against Northampton. Passing is an essential skill that all rugby players must master. Done well, it can move the ball from player to player, without the opposition getting close to the ball.

Putting it all together

While some skills are specific to a position, all rugby players should be able to perform a range of skills that they can use in different circumstances. Forwards may find themselves in the middle of an attacking move and should know how to perform with other players around them. Similarly, backs can find themselves involved at a break-down and should know the laws and skills involved in rucks and mauls. In certain cases, it can be a deliberate tactic to have players standing out of position. For example, a large forward can be standing out in the backs to create a mismatch in size against a smaller opposition back.

> " *I only get the points because I have team-mates who do the work and put me in the position to get them.* "
>
> **Jonny Wilkinson**
> England fly-half

Team training

All players need to practise basic rugby skills such as passing, catching and tackling. However, there are a few skills that only certain players will use during a match.

Individual training

While any player can kick the team's penalty goals, they are usually taken by a back, most often the fly-half. Similarly, while anyone can throw the ball into the lineout, throw-ins are usually performed by the hooker. The fly-half and hooker will practise kicking and throwing in on their own, before bringing these skills together as part of a larger move, such as a lineout.

Players at every level need to practise skills. Here, Jonny Wilkinson practises his penalty kicking. He holds the Rugby World Cup points record (227).

Tactics Tip

While you need to master basic skills, such as catching and passing the ball, you also need to build your general fitness and stamina so that you will last the match's 80 minutes.

Group training

Players also come together in groups to practise larger format skills and the tactics associated with them. For example, a group of forwards will practise scrums, lineouts, rucks and mauls. Then the team will come together to try out different tactics that they can use in a match. They will rehearse these at various levels of intensity. Initially, they will practise a move without any opposition, then they will carry out the move against players carrying tackling shields. Finally, to re-create the conditions of a match, they will practise the move with 'live' opposition, where players will perform proper tackles and try to stop attacking moves.

This team is wearing body padding during a practice session. The pads will protect players from picking up injuries before a match.

Coaches

A team's tactics and training are decided by the coach. Larger clubs and national sides will have a head coach who oversees a team of coaches, each of whom will control a different aspect of play.

Head coach

As well as deciding what overall tactics to use, a head coach will also decide which players start a match. It is usually the head coach's job to study future opposition teams, either on video or by going to watch them play, to find out their tactics. He will use this information to determine what tactics to use against them. The coach will also scout for new players by watching matches played by other teams.

Toulon's Aubin Hueber (left) and Philippe Saint-Andre (right) watch their team closely. Headphones enable them to discuss tactics with support staff up in the stands.

Italy's assistant coach, Alessandro Troncon, watches on while Andrea Marcato takes a penalty kick. The backs coach is responsible for ensuring that the team attacks as a unit and that players use their individual skills, such as kicking, to score points.

Specialist coaches

Some coaches train players for specific roles or parts of a match. Forwards coaches will make sure that the forwards are drilled in scrums, lineouts, rucks and mauls. An attack coach will train all players in attacking moves to suit different situations, while a defensive coach will drill the team to defend in different situations. For example, they may decide to use a rush defence (see pages 14–15) to put pressure on opposition players and force them to make a mistake. In national teams, there are also coaches for very specific roles. For example, a kicking coach will help the team's goal kicker to improve his penalty taking.

> *I treat coaching no differently to parenting.*
>
> **Scott Johnson**
> Ospreys and former Wales coach

Styles of play

Teams can adopt different styles of play depending on the skills of their own players or in response to the tactics used by the opposition.

Keep it tight

If a team has a particularly strong set of forwards, then the coach may decide to use a forward-based, or tight, game. This sees the forwards control most of the team's possession, using rucks and mauls (see pages 18–19) along with short passes to drive back the weaker opposition forwards. Long kicks are also used to put the ball out of play deep in opposition territory. Although this gives the defending side a lineout (see pages 24–25), it gives the forwards the chance to win the lineout and continue an attack.

During a Junior World Rugby Trophy game against Papua New Guinea (in red and black), the Zimbabwe forwards (in green and white) use a driving maul to keep possession and get the ball up the pitch.

Fast and loose

Instead of playing a tight game, teams can choose to play a quick, expansive game using fast, long passes. This style of play can be very effective at stretching defences. It can also expose weaknesses as players frantically chase the ball and try to win possession.

An expansive style of play can be very risky. Long passes can be difficult to throw accurately, especially when defenders are close by. Long passes are also easier for defenders to read. They can spot when an attacker is about to throw one and step forwards to catch or intercept the pass, winning possession.

> **" The aim is to play an expansive and exciting type of rugby (even if the ball doesn't always make it to the wing). "**
>
> **David Strettle**
> England and
> Saracens wing

Scotland's Simon Danielli is tackled by Italy's Antonio Pavanello. Danielli is looking to make a quick pass to stop a break-down forming.

Attacking options

When attacking teams have the ball, their aim is to advance towards the tryline. There are many ways of doing this, depending on the style of play they want to use.

Defence is the best form of attack

Sometimes, a team may choose not to attack at all. Instead, they use a strong defence, allowing the opposition to launch one attack after another. The plan is that the attacking team will eventually make a mistake and lose possession of the ball. This gives the defending team the chance to launch its own fast-paced counter-attack.

BALL IN HAND

Wingers Jonah Lomu and Bryan Habana are joint holders of the record for the most tries in a World Cup. Both have scored eight: Lomu in 1999 and Habana in 2007.

Castre's strong defence has meant that Matemini Masoe can steal possession and launch a counter-attack. His team-mates are rushing to support his attack.

Switch pass

1 The ball carrier suddenly changes direction to run diagonally. His team-mate runs an opposite diagonal line behind the ball carrier.

2 As the players cross, the ball carrier twists and makes a short pass to his team-mate, who can continue the attack.

Pass and run

The simplest attacking tactic is to pass the ball along the line of backs to the wingers. However, this is predictable to defend against. To make attacks more complicated, teams use moves to create gaps in the defence or a situation where attackers outnumber defenders. These include loops and switches. Teams also use dummy runners, who look as if they are going to receive a pass, drawing defenders towards them. Instead, they pass to another player who uses the space left by the tricked defenders.

Loop

1 A loop creates an overlap of attackers. When a team is attacking in a line, the ball carrier passes to the player next to him.

2 Once he has passed the ball, he runs to the end of the attacking line. In the meantime, the player who has caught the ball, passes to the player who is next to him.

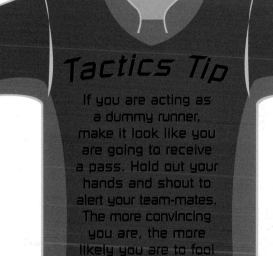

Tactics Tip

If you are acting as a dummy runner, make it look like you are going to receive a pass. Hold out your hands and shout to alert your team-mates. The more convincing you are, the more likely you are to fool the opposition.

Defensive play

When defending, teams look to stop opposition attacks and force the attacking team into making mistakes. Defenders must work as a unit so that there are no gaps for attackers to exploit.

Working as one

Defending teams need to co-ordinate their moves so that they act as a unit. To begin with, defending players will stand in a straight line. This is very important. If a single player stands in front of or behind the defensive line it leaves gaps that attackers can exploit to break the defence.

New Zealand's national team, the All Blacks, form a defensive line behind a maul during a match against Italy. The line ensures that there is plenty of defensive cover.

The Italian national team demonstrates a drift defence in an effort to stop the All Blacks from scoring. In a drift defence, defenders step sideways, following the ball across the pitch and making sure that there are enough defenders to stop the wingers.

Drift or rush?

Once they have formed a defensive line, defenders have a number of tactics they can use. For example, if an attacking team is looking to pass the ball as quickly as possible to its players who are out wide, defenders can choose to use a drift defence. Alternatively, defenders can choose to run up to attackers in a rush or blitz defence. This can put pressure on attackers, forcing them to make a mistake. However, it can be risky as it leaves space behind the defensive line, which a short chip kick can exploit.

The defending team in white rushes at the attackers. This gives the attacking players less time and space and they are forced to play quickly, making it more likely that they will make a mistake.

A kicking game

Kicks can be used in both defensive and attacking situations to move the ball down the pitch to safety or to break an opposition's defence. There are different types of kick that can be used to suit each situation.

Defensive kicks

When players are defending close to their own tryline, a kick down the pitch is a good way to clear their lines. Defenders can kick the ball down the pitch so that the opposition has to run back to field it. While this will give defenders the time to organise a defence, it gives the opposition a chance to launch another attack. Alternatively, the defending players can choose to kick the ball into touch, giving the throw-in at the lineout to the opposition. In both cases, kicking players look to get as much distance on their kick as possible.

The player in blue is under pressure from an opposition attack. To clear the ball, he tries to kick it as far down the pitch as possible. As he kicks the ball, the attacking player tries to block it to gain possession.

Attacking kicks

As well as passing and running, attacking teams can use a range of kicks to break through an opposition's defence. Some kicks send the ball quickly behind the opposition's defence, forcing them to turn and run back. Attacking kicks include box kicks and grubbers, both of which put pressure on the opposition's defence.

Samoa's David Lemy uses a grubber kick to send the ball past the Italian defence. A grubber kick is a short kick that stays low to the ground.

A box kick is a high kick taken out of a player's hands. The attackers can chase the kick to put pressure on the opposition.

Rucks and mauls

Once a player has been tackled, both teams will try to win possession during the break-down. If the tackled player is brought to the floor, then a ruck may form, but if the players stay on their feet, a maul will form.

Quick or slow?

Teams that favour playing a fast-paced game will look to spend as little time as possible at the break-down. They will want to move the ball away quickly so that defending teams have little time to organise a defence. If teams want to play a slower game, they may choose to use driving mauls. These can be very effective at drawing in defenders who try to stop the maul moving forwards. When enough defenders have been drawn in, this can create gaps for the attacking backs to exploit.

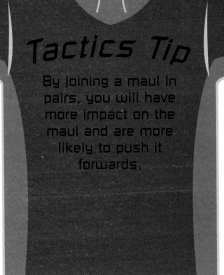

Tactics Tip

By joining a maul in pairs, you will have more impact on the maul and are more likely to push it forwards.

With a strong set of forwards, France use a driving maul to secure possession during a game against Argentina.

Perpignan's Nicolas Laharrague looks to make a short pass from the back of a ruck. This short pass will draw in the Stade Toulousain defenders (in red) and create gaps on the pitch that the attackers can exploit.

Defending teams

Defending players will look to slow down how quickly a ball can be removed from a ruck or maul. This gives them time to organise their own defence. They will also try to do this with as few players as possible. Committing a lot of players to defending a break-down means that there are fewer defenders standing out wide, leaving gaps that attackers could exploit.

To slow down an attack, defenders try to get their hands on the ball. However, they need to listen to the referee. Handling the ball in a ruck is illegal and can lead to a defending player being penalised, giving away a penalty to the opposition.

> *You can suck in defenders by mauling and hitting off the sides and staying on your feet.*
>
> **Jeremy Guscott**
> Former England, Lions and Bath centre

Changing tactics

During a match, players need to study how successful their tactics are and where their own weaknesses are. Players should also look for weaknesses in the opposition.

Spotting a weakness

From the very first whistle, players will look to see which of the opposition players may be strong or weak at a particular ability, such as tackling or running. For example, if there is one opposition player who is a strong runner, then a team may decide that there should always be two tacklers on that player whenever he gets the ball. Opposition teams can be weak during set-pieces, such as scrums and lineouts. If the opposition has a weak lineout, then the attacking team can exploit this by kicking the ball out of play, hoping that they will win the lineout.

BALL IN HAND

During a 2003 Rugby World Cup match, Australia made history when they exploited a weak Namibian team to win 142-0.

The mismatch in size between these two players means that the attacking team will try to ensure that they are always running at the smaller player.

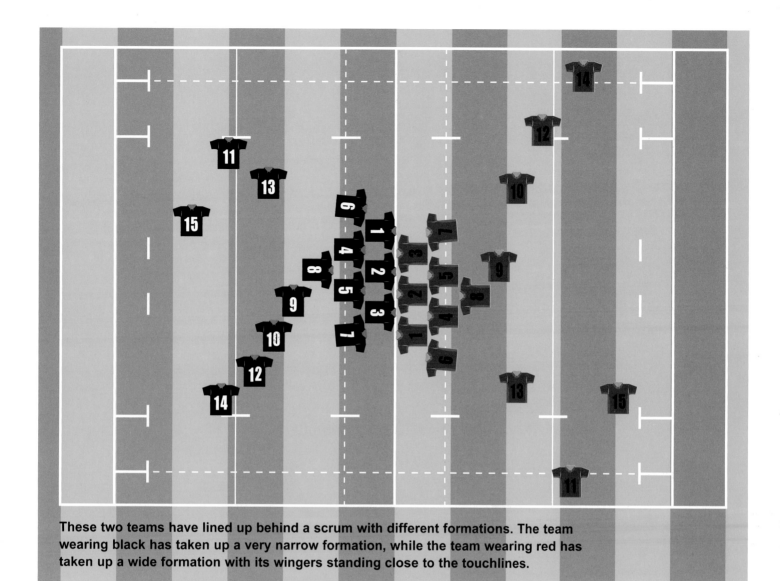

These two teams have lined up behind a scrum with different formations. The team wearing black has taken up a very narrow formation, while the team wearing red has taken up a wide formation with its wingers standing close to the touchlines.

Tactics Tip

Listen carefully to the instructions coming from your captain or coach during a match. They may change your team's tactics at any moment and you may need to change the way you play.

Wide or narrow

By studying where the opposition's strengths and weaknesses are, teams may also decide to alter their formation. For example, if the opposition has strong attacking runners that are being brought up the middle of the pitch, then a defending team will line up in a narrower formation so that more players are in the centre of the pitch. Alternatively, an attacking team that spots that the opposition has taken such a narrow formation, may choose to send its wingers out wide where they will be unopposed.

At the scrum

Scrums offer an attacking team a good opportunity to punch holes in the opposition defence. With both sets of forwards tied up in the scrum, there may be lots of space for the backs to launch an attack.

Launching an attack

Even with the forwards committed to a Scrum, opposition players can still run up quickly to defend, while quick, back row players can stop an attack. To counter this, attacking teams may play a move close to a scrum. This can include the scrum-half making a short pass to a player running near the scrum or the number eight picking up the ball from the back of the scrum and running with it. This tactic commits defending back row players to making a tackle. It will also stop any other defenders from rushing up too quickly.

Perpignan's number eight, Henry Tuilagi, has picked up the ball from the back of the scrum and is running with it. This move will keep the defending back row players close to the scrum as they try to stop him.

The team in blue has been awarded a scrum close to the opposition tryline. They have chosen to go for a pushover try. The players need to push the ball over the tryline so that the scrum-half or number eight can touch the ball down.

Going for it

When an attacking team is awarded a free-kick or penalty, it can choose to take a scrum. This can be a good option as it commits opposition forwards to the scrum and stops them standing out wide to defend against attacks.

If a team has a very strong scrum and the penalty is awarded close to the opposition's tryline, then the attacking side may choose to go for a pushover try.

Tactics Tip

Binding properly is very important in good scrummaging because it gives the forwards a more solid base from which to push. If the front row does not bind properly, the scrum will be less powerful.

Lineouts

Like scrums, lineouts offer attacking teams a good chance to secure possession and launch an attack.

Catch and drive

When choosing what to do in a lineout, attacking teams have to know their own strengths, as well as the strengths and weaknesses of the opposition. For example, if the opposition has a very strong set of forwards, it would be wrong to try to set up a maul straight from a lineout – the attacking team would just get pushed back, or could lose possession. Instead, attacking players may choose to move the ball away from the lineout quickly. The jumper will tap the ball back to the scrum-half who will then make a quick pass to the backs.

Catch and drive

The team in blue has chosen to set up a driving maul from the lineout. Once the ball is caught, the forwards rush to form the maul around the catcher.

Here, the team in blue has chosen to clear the ball away from the lineout as quickly as possible. Instead of catching the ball, the jumper (second from the front) taps the ball out to the scrum-half.

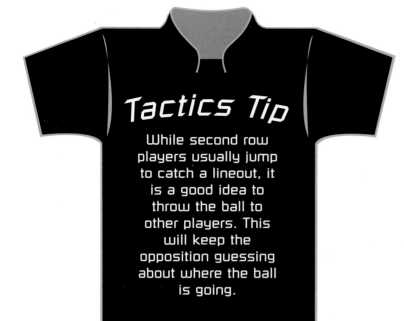

Tactics Tip

While second row players usually jump to catch a lineout, it is a good idea to throw the ball to other players. This will keep the opposition guessing about where the ball is going.

Mixing it up

Most lineouts involve both sets of forwards. However, the laws of rugby allow for any number of players to stand in a lineout, so long as there are at least two from each team. Teams that have been awarded the lineout decide how many players stand in the lineout, and the opposition must have the same number of players or fewer. As such, teams can choose to have fewer players – known as a shortened lineout. This gives their jumpers more room in which to catch the throw-in.

This shortened lineout has two players from each side. Although the shortened lineout is harder to defend, it gives the attacking team more room to catch the ball. It also means that the attacking team has players ready to pass the ball out to gain possession.

Using substitutes

A team is not just made up of the 15 players on the pitch, it also includes extra players, or substitutes. Substitutes are used to replace injured or tired players or to change tactics.

Substitute laws

In games for younger players rolling substitutions are allowed. Teams can change players whenever they want to and players are allowed to come off and go back onto the pitch. At senior level, there must be enough substitutes trained to replace the front row. If there are not enough of these players, then the referee will insist on uncontested scrums to protect players from injury. During these, teams cannot push against each other and hookers cannot strike the ball to steal possession.

BALL IN HAND

A temporary substitute can come onto the pitch to replace a bleeding player. If the bleeding player is off the pitch for more than 15 minutes, then the replacement will be permanent.

These players are waiting on the bench. At top-level matches, eight substitutions are allowed. Once a player has been replaced, he cannot return to the pitch, unless it is to replace a bleeding player.

Changing the game

Teams can use substitutes to change the way they play the game. For example, a team struggling in defence may opt to bring on a large back-line player to help stop the opposition. If a team is struggling at the break-down, a second-row forward could be substituted by a back-row forward in order to make the pack more mobile. Alternatively, if a penalty kicker is struggling to hit the target, then he may be replaced with another kicker who is among the substitutes.

Tactics Tip

If you are a substitute, it is important that you stretch and warm-up regularly during the match. That way, you will be ready to step onto the pitch at a moment's notice.

If a team is losing, the coach may decide to substitute a tired back. He would hope that the substitute will have the energy to launch an attack and add to the scoreline.

Team spirit

Playing as a unit is vital to being successful. Teams that are not organised and players who do not play as a team, are likely to leave gaps in their defence that the opposition can exploit.

> *The whole point of rugby is that it is, first and foremost, a state of mind, a spirit.*
>
> **Jean-Pierre Rives**
> Former French player

Communication

Before a game, players should discuss tactics so that everyone in the team knows what they have to do during different situations. During a match, it is very important for players to talk to each other. They should let their team-mates know where they are when supporting a runner. They should also tell their team-mates who has the ball, especially in a maul when the ball can be difficult to spot.

Players from Stade Toulousain stand in a huddle before a match. The captain will use the huddle to encourage his team-mates to play as a unit and to discuss tactics.

Standing just behind a maul, the scrum-half can clearly see where his own players and the opposition players are standing.

Encouragement

Captains play a very important role in keeping a team's morale up, especially if they are losing. Part of a captain's job is to talk to team-mates, encouraging them to play better or not to worry about a mistake they may have made. Scrum-halves also have a very important role in encouraging and guiding players during a match. They act as the link between the forwards and backs. Because they stand just behind a ruck, maul, lineout or scrum, they have a very good view of where all the players are on the pitch. From this position, they can tell their own forwards where to go to block any holes in a defence.

What it takes to be...

A top coach

Pierre Berbizier

After his retirement as a top player for France, Pierre Berbizier was made head coach of the French national side. Under his leadership, the team made it to the semi-finals of the 1995 World Cup. Since then, he has coached French clubs and the Italian national team.

Career path

- 1981 Makes his debut playing for France aged 22.

- 1991 Plays in his last game for France.

- 1992 Made French head coach.

- 1995 Leaves position as French head coach.

- 1998 Coaches French club RC Narbonne. Leaves this post in 2001.

- 2005 Appointed head coach of Italy.

- 2007 Italy win two matches in the Six Nations for the first time.

- 2007 Leaves Italy to coach Racing Métro 92 Paris.

A successful career saw Pierre win more than 50 caps for his country. He captained France to a Grand Slam in 1987 and a runners-up spot at the first Rugby World Cup played that year.

Glossary

All Blacks the nickname for New Zealand's national rugby team.

backs the group of seven players who line up behind the forwards and are involved in attacking moves.

break-down the period immediately after a tackle has been made.

British and Irish Lions a collection of players from England, Scotland, Wales and Ireland that makes up a touring side.

dummy a technique where a player pretends to perform a move to trick a defender.

formation the way a team lines up. For example, in a wide formation, the wingers will be out towards the touchlines.

forwards the group of eight players who are involved in scrums and lineouts.

Grand Slam when a team playing in the Six Nations wins all its games.

intercept to catch the ball as it is passed from one opposition player to another.

off-load get rid of the ball, usually by passing, as a tackle is made.

possession when a team has the ball.

set-piece restart moves such as lineouts and scrums.

Six Nations the annual tournament that takes place between the national teams of England, Ireland, Wales, Scotland, France and Italy.

Books

Training to Succeed: Rugby by Rita Story (Franklin Watts, 2009)
Sporting Skills: Rugby by Clive Gifford (Wayland, 2008)
Inside Sport: Rugby by Clive Gifford (Wayland, 2007)

Websites

www.aru.rugby.com.au/onlinecoaching
The online coaching pages of the Australian Rugby Union's website are full of lessons, drills and tips to improve skills.

www.planet-rugby.com
An international website with coverage of leagues, cups and national teams from all over the world.

Index